skin deep

KRISTINA CARTER

EDITED BY
NICOLE QUEEN

VISION PUBLISHING
HOUSE

To all those who believe in the power of love, unity, and the boundless potential of the human heart. May you be inspired to see beyond the surface, embrace diversity, and cultivate a world where every shade of skin is celebrated as a unique masterpiece in the grand tapestry of humanity.

contents

Lord, I pray that Your will be done through this book. I am humbled that You would employ me in this manner.

Lord, You said in Your Word that we cannot serve two masters; we must either hate one or love the other. Thus, Lord, today we declare our love for You, our sister, brother, neighbor, family, and ourselves. You stated in Your word that love covers a multitude of sins and that whoever is without sin should cast the first stone.

Lord, I thank You for Your boundless love for this planet, which You came to save. We are thankful that You came to save the sinful guy. Your love is so unconditional and faultless that it cannot be quantified or lessened.

Your love, Lord, has drawn me out of the world and into Your presence. I would not be alive if it hadn't been for Your love. Because of Your love for me, I can now love my adversaries. Your love is incredible. Your love has changed my life. We'd be lost without You.

I thank You, Lord, for Your mercy and grace! Everything I've gone through has prepared me for my mission. Father, You have an evident purpose! Lord Jesus, I adore You because You are LOVE!

Lord, use me for Your purposes in this book. I pray that this book changes the world and that people take stock of their life, how they think, and how they treat those around them. For You have said in Your Word that whoever offends even one of my children has done it unto me.

Oh Lord, please assist us. As a nation, culture, people, and individuals, we need You, God. Lord, I beseech You to do Your will on earth as it is in heaven!

I pray for a huge transformation, complete turnaround, healing of minds and hearts, spiritual wisdom, knowledge, and insight, and deliverance in Jesus' Name!

We can't accomplish anything without You, Lord! We can't live without You since it's Your love that makes us love! Hallelujah! Glory to Your name, God!

Jesus, You are amazing, mighty, and an astounding marvel in my life! Thank You, Lord, for being the love that I need to show others. Without it, I couldn't love as much as I do!

You are the Almighty God, and I praise Your Holy Name! In Jesus' Name I pray, Amen.

introduction

When I observe the evil occurring in the world, my heart sometimes feels heavy. People being abused because of their skin color hurts my heart. Therefore, I hope this book opens people's eyes, removes the wool from their eyes, opens their minds, and regulates and punctures (if not, softens) their hardened hearts.

I assure you that I come from a state of love, peace, and compassion. I was led to write this book by the Holy Spirit. It's a subject that I'm passionate about. A prophet's heart is always burdened with something the Lord has placed on their heart for them to deal with on earth. Although I write from a place of love, some parts of this book are intended to demolish the devil's playground and annihilate every plot, plan, and scheme of the spirit of racism. As a result, it may come across as a little blunt, direct, or even harsh. However, the Holy Spirit has called me to this, and I am anointed and purposed for this battle.

My entire life has prepared me for this war, and the Lord has equipped me for such a moment. I adore individuals regardless of their skin color. I was born in Memphis, Tennessee, and grew up in White Haven until I was twelve years old. The majority of the residents in the area were African Americans. At the time, there were just three Caucasian households in the area. Growing up in and around the

African American community, that culture seemed to be natural to me.

I feel quite at ease in the presence of African Americans. I am currently married to an African American guy, and I have three adult children— two from my first marriage and one from my second. My third child is multiracial. I have six grandkids; four of them are biracial. I am concerned about their future and deeply adore them. I've trained my children to appreciate individuals for who they are, not what they look like, or the color of their skin.

Skin color is never brought up in our family talks; it's simply not something we discuss. We don't waste time on frivolous pursuits. I have always instructed my children to play with the child on the playground who is alone and with whom no one else is playing. This is what they have done since they were children. I have taught my children to fight for what is right, to prioritize God, and to love others.

I am a prayerful mother who has taught her children to pray because prayer changes things. I hope this book will alter how we, as God's people, look at others in this world.

I understand how an African American feels. A mother feels a sense of loss when her son leaves the house. I understand because I have a multiracial son, and I pray for him every time he leaves the home, that God would cover him with His blood and send His warrior angels to keep him safe. We shouldn't have to feel that way every time our boys leave the house, whether it's to go to the grocery store, work, or simply hang out with friends. I've had the same conversation with him about the risks in our society that African American mothers have with their boys.

My son is well aware that he is classified as a black guy in our culture and that he may face danger just because of his skin color. However, he also knows God, is saved, and understands how to pray for God's protection. Yes, we should pray and believe God to protect us regularly, but not just because we have individuals in our society who are meant to protect and serve, yet occasionally abuse the law.

A badge does not entitle someone to act as judge, jury, or executioner. Honor, dignity, honesty, good character, and safety should all be emblazoned on a badge! My father was a cop in Memphis, Tennessee; therefore, I'm not going after all cops. Every precinct, he said, has crooked officers. I recall him urging me not to stop for an officer on a dark road; instead, he advised me to go to a police station, if necessary, when I suspected that an officer was up to no good. Cops are humans, and they, too, might have heart problems. They are human, just like you and me.

Racism is a spirit that may be possessed by anyone. Anyone can be acting in a racist manner. It's unfortunate that a black youngster cannot trust a police officer to whom they may have to flee someday. How can they believe them, given what they've seen on television and in real-time? We live in a country that declares, "In God we trust." We live in a country where innocence is declared unless proven guilty! *Lies*!

When it comes down to it, many people, including officers, assess young black males based on their appearance. They may be viewed as perpetrators of crime.

People cannot change their appearance, such as skin color; they are born with certain qualities. I'll simply say it: in our nation, we preach God, innocence, and liberty for all! However, those are lies! The devil is a deceiver!

I will oppose every spirit of darkness that opposes God's people. With the Blood of Jesus, I take on the spirit of racism! I'm not afraid to speak up against the enemy! God did not give me a fearful spirit! In Jesus' tremendous Name, we must summon this demon and deal with it! I have faith in God to keep my son safe!

It's time to go to war for our children!

check your bias

Racism is the conviction that one race is superior to another, often leading to discrimination and prejudice against people based on race or ethnicity.

 Then Peter spoke out, saying, "I understand that God is not a respecter of persons: God sees no male or female."

ACTS 10:34

God examines our hearts rather than our physical color. There is no such thing as a Jew or a Gentile, a slave or a free person, or a male or a female person in Christ Jesus. This encapsulates everything! God doesn't care if you're a man or a woman; he doesn't distinguish between them. As a result, when we join the family of Jesus Christ, we become one Spirit, one body, one faith, one religion, and one in Christ. We are delivered from our sins when we receive salvation.

Racism is a criminal offense. Racism cannot be combated by racism! Racism is an evil spirit! We must understand that God detests this.

1

He is our Creator, Redeemer, and Savior. As a result, we fall victim to witchcraft if we believe we are superior to a group of individuals who aren't like us. We are the Jezebels and practice witchcraft if we believe this lie. How can we assume we're better than Jesus when he doesn't care about who he's talking to? How can we think one is better than the other if Jesus doesn't think so? *God, please help us!*

Take a long, hard look at how you treat others and yourself. Don't you desire to hear God say, "Well done, good and faithful servant?" You don't want to hear, "Go away from me! I had no idea who you were!"

We are not acting in the love of Jesus Christ when we treat others badly and are judgmental and harsh to them. You cannot abuse someone and be alright with it if you are genuinely saved and have submitted to the Holy Spirit! The Holy Spirit will convict you to return to that individual and get it right. The Holy Spirit, prayer, and God's Word are essential for leading a holy life.

I thank God for Jesus, and I honestly don't know what I would do if I didn't have the Holy Spirit to lead and guide me. I would be completely lost! Godly wisdom and understanding are required when living in this world and fighting our daily spiritual struggle!

I pray that God's children awaken for it's a pity to be in God's kingdom, yet defeated! You need to establish a personal relationship with God. Don't wait for others to pray for you; start with yourself.

The Lord is waiting for your response! He yearns for a close relationship with you! God, Jesus, and the Holy Spirit are all real! God's Word is alive and thriving!

 A new command I give you: Love one another, as I have loved you, so you must love one another.

JOHN 13:34 KJV

This Scripture states to love one another— not just to love just black people as society calls black love, or to love only white people as society calls white love— but to love one another! There is no such thing as black love, white love, black power, or white power in God; thus, we better attempt to obtain the Holy Spirit's power to adore each other! The Bible says that without Him, we can do nothing; thus, we need Him to love correctly, love without borders, love without color, love without prejudices, love without stereotypes, and love without limits in Jesus' mighty Name!

God's love is *terrifying*! God's Word is *extremely effective*! Therefore, I speak. Love is capable of covering a wide range of sins. All is conquered by love. Jesus is the personification of love.

MOMENT OF REFLECTION

Romans 2:11 says, "For there is no respect of persons with God." Meditate on this truth and journal what God reveals to you.

_____

_____

_____

_____

_____

_____

_____

_____

_____

_____

_____

_____

_____

_____

_____

_____

_____

examine your heart

Racism, prejudice, and discrimination are heart issues, not black-or-white issues! The heart is corrupt and evil, and nothing good comes from it. We've got to get our act together. We must get our hearts and minds in the proper place and order! Become obedient to God's Word! Be whole.

It is not your concern how people view you. It's none of your business how someone feels about you since they see you through the eyes of their heart. Life's challenges originate from our hearts; it's a cardiac problem. That is something we must understand. People behave and respond based on their feelings. It's a problem with the heart. There is nothing good in our flesh! We must fight in the spirit!

 And those who are in the flesh cannot please God.

ROMANS 8:8 KJV

Listen, I came to destroy the devil's playground, yet some of you assist him regularly by allowing hatred to take root in your hearts. We should not be guided by our emotions when we are out and about.

Our emotions will sometimes cause us to be all over the place. We must be steady in all aspects of our lives.

With our emotions, we can't serve God! We must worship Him in Spirit and truth! We don't walk by sight but by faith! We conduct our lives based on faith, not on our feelings. Hallelujah!

My faith is something I thank and adore God for! It's time for us to pull ourselves together. We must correct our hearts! Let's get our heads in the game! Adhere to God's Word! Be whole and be smart, beloved.

Were you ever attacked by someone with a racist attitude? I'm sure many of us have been. However, no matter what occurred, we still cannot combat a racist spirit with the flesh; we'll always lose.

God has strategically positioned me in society so that I may observe both sides of this heart attitude and its impact on our society. White people criticize Black people, and Black people criticize White people. Unarmed Black people are having their lives taken by officers of the law. Police shootings tend to occur in waves, followed by a pause. That is unquestionably the enemy! We must recognize that God is envious! We should not serve the enemy through hatred, bigotry, racism, etc.

 And envy, drunkenness, carousing, and the like, I warn you, as I did before, that those who practice such things will not inherit the kingdom of God. But the fruit of the Spirit is love, joy, peace, patience, kindness, goodness, faithfulness, gentleness, and self-control. Against such things, there is no law.

GALATIANS 5:22 KJV

God is not a liar. His word is trustworthy, and it will come to pass. We're deceiving ourselves if we think we're being honest with God while still hating others. That is witchcraft. That isn't God's doing! God is all about love, as He is love. We must become like Jesus Christ.

Love is patient, love is kind, and is not jealous; love does not brag and is not arrogant.

1 CORINTHIANS 13:4 KJV

MOMENT OF REFLECTION

James 4:8 says, "Draw near to God and He will draw near to you, cleanse your hands, you sinners, and purify your hearts, you double-minded." Meditate on this truth and journal what God reveals to you.

_____

_____

_____

_____

_____

_____

_____

_____

_____

_____

_____

_____

_____

_____

_____

_____

_____

_____

_____

_____

_____

_____

_____

evaluate your distinctions

Owning your own business is fantastic, but it doesn't need to be mentioned that it's a black-owned firm. Why? Because that is a racist statement. I've seen conversations on Facebook that go something like, "Are you a black-owned business?" And they responded 'yes.' The consumer would not have bought from them if they had said 'no.' That is a racist attitude— point blank. Any form of division that offends is bad, and it is not from God. I understand racism and how it operates, but we cannot allow it to offend our souls and cause us to be divided in every aspect of our lives.

Yes, Blacks should own their enterprises, but it is unnecessary to specify that they are black-owned. Race has nothing to do with money. We would lose our blessings if we just sell to the Black community. God may have someone of a different nationality weave into our businesses. However, if we separate ourselves from individuals who do not look like us, we shut ourselves off from the possibility of its benefits.

Isolating from other races is completely absurd. I want people of all nationalities to conduct business with me! I will not shut off God's blessings by being racist and acting offensively. When we detest an entire race because of the color of their skin, we miss out on beautiful connections with amazing individuals. I'm not sure why we think it's okay to dislike someone just because of who they are; they were made by God, not by themselves.

 Know ye that the Lord he is God: it is he that hath made us, and not we: we are his people and the sheep of his pasture.

PSALM 100:3 KJV

MOMENT OF REFLECTION

John 15:4-6 says, "Abide in me, and I in you, as the branch cannot bear fruit by itself, unless it abides in the vine, neither can you, unless you abide in me. I am the vine; you are the branches." Meditate on this truth and journal what God reveals to you.

_____
_____
_____
_____
_____
_____
_____
_____
_____
_____
_____
_____
_____
_____
_____

build your
connections

R acism is an evil spirit. It is demonic and has been sent to divide, conquer, hate, rip down, kill, steal, and destroy. Living in God's peace and walking in love allows you to live better, treat people better, exhibit love, and reveal Jesus to others! Don't hold onto bitterness. Turn the page and let it go! Don't let it destroy your connections.

We are stronger when we work together and weaker when we work alone. If we banded together, we could demolish every plot, plan, and scheme that the adversary attempts to impose on God's people. Cancer could be eradicated if we all work together. We have the potential to eradicate a mental disease if we work together. We can put a stop to human trafficking if we work together. We can eradicate poverty if we work together. We can defeat drug addiction and alcoholism if we work together. We can defeat the spirits of suicide, sadness, anxiety, and bullying if we band together! We can defeat the spirit of racism if we work together!

We can do it if we come together!

The adversary depends on our disunity! That's why he offers us mental recommendations. That's why he says you're better than someone else, which causes strife. If we are separated, we are not united. The battleground is our thoughts! The adversary can have us bound if he can gain our thoughts!

If we aren't operating in unity, then we will many of the miracles of Jesus! If we aren't touching and agreeing with Him and His Word, then what are we doing? There has never been a time in American history when the country has been more divided than it is today. It's time to come together and change the narrative!

The enemy is running rampant all around us. The devil is making an appearance at the White House. He is attacking our schools— murdering our students and teachers. Sexual perversion is rampant in today's culture. Human trafficking is the work of the enemy. The devil also manifests himself through our young, who are addicted to narcotics and are murdering one another on the streets. Our children are resorting to drugs because being high provides them with some respite. They should be able to turn to their moms and fathers for comfort, but they are sometimes part of the problem, so they turn to a fast cure.

We need to pray for our youth to come to faith in Jesus because they are searching for a way to fill a need in their hearts that only Jesus can fill. In Jesus' Name, we can put an end to this street life epidemic; we can demolish it and send it back to the pits of hell from where it came!

 Behold, I give you power, to tread on serpents, and scorpions, and overall, the power of the enemy.

LUKE 10:19 KJV

The weapon will arise, but it will not flourish, according to the Bible. Every day, we must believe and proclaim God's word over our lives and our children's lives. This is the power of unity!

When we come together, we can destroy the enemy's camp.

However, when one group of people dislikes another group of people, that group begins to resent the group that hates them, and it causes disunity. Can't we see what's truly going on in the spirit realm? The devil, our opponent, is banking on it; we are assisting him in killing, stealing, and destroying. When we dislike people and are cruel to them, we perform the enemy's work! I've even observed prejudice behind the pulpit in church—in God's home! There was racism at the temple of God!

We are all human and must answer for our actions. Jesus came to Earth and paid the high price for our sins on the Cross so that we might live free from the enemy's tactics, condemnation, the agony of death, and sin. How can we be free, but at the same time, lock up individuals who don't look, act, or dress like us? How can we claim to be free, while putting someone else in prison?

Let's look at this from a spiritual level. We may want to hold people captive because of how they treat us, but Jesus wants to free us. Who are we to stop that? When it comes to rescuing and releasing people, God does not show bias. Those with a personal relationship with God can access His favor. Jesus came to redeem the entire world, not just a select few! Therefore, we must realize that we are not superior to the next person because of our appearance or skin color. To believe in this superiority is to be completely ignorant of God's truth.

MOMENT OF REFLECTION

Philippians 2:3 says, "Do nothing from selfishness or empty conceit, but with humility of mind regard one another as more important than you." Meditate on this truth and journal what God reveals to you.

_____

_____

_____

_____

cleanse your heart

The Gospel is the Good News of Jesus Christ! So many people have sad hearts because they blame themselves for their sins and try to work off its penalties in the church. We can't pay for our sins since Jesus already paid the price.

We are turning our backs on what Jesus did on the Cross when we try to pay for our sins or walk around carrying them in our bosoms—feeding them, clinging on to them, and enabling them to keep us captive. The devil, not Jesus, is the one who condemns!

In Jesus' Name, I come against the spirits of intimidation, bullying, racism, self-exaltation, and haughtiness. In Jesus' Name, I replace it with humility and sever it from our lives. In Christ Jesus, we are one! Amen!

No one requires the approval of another person. You and I are both validated by Jesus! He is all the proof we'll ever require. We allow others too much control over us and our minds. Racism is a heinous crime. Although Jesus despises sin, He adores you.

 No longer will each man teach his neighbor or his brother, saying, Know the Lord, because they will all know me, from the least of them to the greatest,

17

declares the Lord. For I will forgive either iniquity and will remember their sins no more.

JEREMIAH 31:34 YLT

We were built with a purpose in mind and for a purpose! We were made to be the people we are in Christ Jesus! He is the Creator, and we are the creatures He has created. We did not beg to be formed. We did not choose our family, nationality, the color of our skin, or the socioeconomic level into which we were born. We were made and put in our mother's womb to be born for God's intended purpose. He has a plan for every one of us, and His will must be carried out in our lives.

It is not His intention that we should despise one another because of the color of our skin. It is not His intention for us to carry enmity for anybody. Let us push ourselves to love one another and accept people for who they are since it is not a choice!

We didn't select Him; He chose us! When will we realize that we were here on this planet for His glory? It's all about His glory, not our feelings or our ideas about what people should or shouldn't be. Get genuine with yourself and accept that it's not about you, me, or them; it's about Jesus, His Glory, and His purpose for our life!

Take stock of your heart and ask God to cleanse it of everything that isn't like Him. And do it with sincerity! Some of us cannot understand our mission because we are fixated on others rather than the Lord! We're too preoccupied with observing what others are doing, who they are doing it with, and how long they have been doing it!

What are your plans? We should seek instruction from our Creator, our Father, and the Holy Spirit so that we do not have to go in circles seeking our mission. He isn't trying to keep your mission a secret from you! Your mission is inside you, but you must have a close connection with the Lord for Him to assist you in discovering it. He is the only one who is aware of your ultimate purpose and identity.

It's a waste of time pointing out flaws in others when there are flaws in yourself. Be comfortable in your skin and with yourself because when you aren't happy, you behave out, and your sadness spills over onto others. And when you rebel against individuals because of differences, it's because you're unhappy with yourself.

This is a personal path for everyone, and we all have issues to work through.

Being unkind to others and mistreating people will not make you feel better about yourself; instead, it will bring you sadness. Being racist and prejudiced is the equivalent of being a bully. How can we advise our children not to bully and then turn around and bully someone just because they aren't like us? It is time to mature and go on with purpose!

We should strive to have God's heart and thoughts at all times. This will help us pray for others while going through challenging times, ourselves! It will enable us to appreciate the beauty in others.

We all have various colors, shapes, and sizes, much like flowers in a flower garden. A lovely garden is made up of a variety of plants. We require diversity in this world; else, it would be a monotonous place to live.

God knows best, understands what we require, and is the Creator of all things. I dare not oppose Him or His handiwork! He has a grand plan for His Kingdom and us! The Holy Spirit desires that we modify our way of thinking. He desires that we refresh our minds with God's Word. That is our truth: we are what we think.

MOMENT OF REFLECTION

Philippians 2:5 says, "Let this mind be in you which was also in Christ Jesus." Meditate on this truth and journal what God reveals to you.

_____

_____

_____

_____

break generational curses

N o one can stop us from achieving our goals, ambitions, visions, and aspirations, but ourselves! No individual— white or black— will be able to stop you from achieving your objectives! Our fate rests in our own hands! What steps do you intend to take? What visions do you have for the future? What kind of dreams do you have?

Stop stating that this or that person is preventing you from moving. They are not preventing you from moving. You are stopping you! This has nothing to do with color! Your fate is not determined by your skin tone! Your fate is inextricably linked to your mindset. What a man thinks is what he is. Whatever you believe is who you are!

Jesus died on the Cross not only for you and me, but for the entire world! Everyone alive and breathing can experience salvation and all of its advantages. We are covered by Jesus' Blood if we accept Him as our Lord and Savior. We are safe because He is watching over us. We cannot be killed by our adversary. Mercy and grace will be with us for the rest of our lives! If we live by faith rather than sight, we are the offspring of Jesus Christ and heirs to His reign, benefits, and promises. Nobody can stop us!

God's will for our life— whatever it may be— will always reign supreme! His plans will always be carried out! No one can stop its fulfillment! *Never underestimate God's power!*

We must maintain a close connection with the Holy Spirit. Prayer is vital; it represents a two-way dialogue between you and the Holy Spirit. In the name of Jesus, seek divine wisdom and insight. This practice should begin even before birth; as soon as we learn we are expecting a child, we should commence praying for their well-being.

To embark on His journey to the Cross, Jesus chose Mary's womb to come into the world as a vulnerable baby in the flesh. It all begins within the womb. Every day and night, earnestly pray for your unborn children and your offspring. Remember that our words hold power; what we declare becomes a part of our reality. Once spoken, our words cannot be retracted, whether they are positive or negative.

The Bible encourages us to maintain a consistent prayer life. Stay vigilant and committed to prayer. Pray for your children's future, and that they may find the life partner God has intended for them, sparing them from the heartache and wasted time that comes with wrong choices in relationships. It shouldn't matter what race or ethnicity their future partners are. Our aim is to shield them from unnecessary pain, heartbreak, and divorce.

Our prayers are heard by God. Pray for your children's lives, speaking blessings, favor, and God's promises over them. Instill in them the habit of praying regularly. Teach them to cultivate a personal connection with the Holy Spirit, bring them to church, and proclaim God's Word over them in Jesus' name. This is how we help our children break free from negative cycles.

Allow the Breaker to shatter those cycles in Jesus' Name! Show them the importance of a prayerful life so they can learn how to commune with the Lord. Above all, teach your children to love unconditionally, for God is love. I challenge you to declare God's word over your life daily, as it holds tremendous power.

Behavior is learned, values and morals are instilled, and prejudice is perpetuated through generations. When will we break free from the cycle of generational curses perpetuated by family members who lack purity in their hearts before God? Just because your parents followed a certain path doesn't mean you must, as well. Let us break the chains of generational curses!

Fix it! Breaker, break it! In Christ, there is no condemnation when we accept Him as our Father and Redeemer. He forgives and forgets our past transgressions. Praise God! Who are we to judge others based on their failures to meet our expectations or the color of their skin?

By the power of Jesus' Blood, I sever such judgments from your life. Hallelujah! I rebuke and bind these judgments. They have no authority in the Name of Jesus!

What will it take for us to realize that we must eliminate certain things from our lives so that our children do not inherit our problems? Racism is a dark stain passed down through generations. Racism is vile, satanic, hateful, and not of God. It destroys love, peace, self-esteem, and the sense of being enough.

With the cleansing power of Jesus' Blood, I confront the spirit of racism! Racism will exploit any ethnic group against another, regardless of their background. The spirit of racism itself is not discriminatory. I urge you to understand the true nature of racism: it is a malevolent, demonic spirit!

MOMENT OF REFLECTION

Galatians 3:28 says, "There is neither Jew nor Gentile, neither slave nor free, nor is there male and female, for you are all one in Christ Jesus." Meditate on this truth and journal what God reveals to you.

_____

_____

_____

_____

_____

_____

confront the spirit of witchcraft

T he adversary is attempting to sow discord and division among us by inciting riots and stirring up tensions between different ethnic groups. The goal is to create an illusion that all whites are against blacks, but we must recognize that this is a tactic by the enemy to cause strife in our society. The devil aims to spark a race war.

It's essential to remember that we are all members of the human race, and whether we like it or not, we are interconnected. This is not a battle based on race; it's a spiritual struggle.

We are indeed in the midst of a conflict, but it's not a racial one. This battle takes place in the spiritual realm, and the adversaries are not defined by their skin color. It's a battle between God's Kingdom children and the forces of darkness.

To effectively combat anything, we must first understand who our true adversary is and how to engage in the fight. This understanding is crucial to win the war!

 The weapons of our warfare are not carnal but mighty in God for pulling down strongholds, casting down arguments and every high thing that exalts itself against the knowledge of God, bringing every thought into captivity to the obedience of Christ, and being ready to punish.

2 CORINTHIANS 10:4–6 KJV

Racism is a battle of the soul! It has nothing to do with carnality. It is religious. It must be battled with the spiritual rather than the physical. Racism cannot be defeated with racism!

Engaging in acts of violence, murder, and physical confrontation will not bring an end to this conflict. Racism cannot be defeated through physical means. The true instigator of this strife is not each other, but the devil himself. We should redirect our focus toward him.

The adversary preys on our pride, encouraging us to prioritize our own interests and ethnic identities. He plants seeds of abuse, mistreatment, and prejudice in our minds, fostering negative and selfish thoughts.

Offense is a spiritual affliction. The adversary seeks to entangle us in a life filled with offense, convincing us that people treat us unfairly and harbor ill feelings toward us. Consider this: not everyone liked Jesus, yet He remained unoffended. He stayed committed to His mission on Earth, undeterred by the adversary's attempts to hinder Him.

Giving in to offense can lead to bitterness, causing anger toward anyone who doesn't acknowledge us or meet our expectations. We must recognize that the spirit of offense corrodes the fruits of the spirit and contaminates our own spirits. The adversary may whisper that others dislike us or intentionally snub us, but the reality might be that they simply didn't notice or had their own reasons for not engaging with us.

The adversary is a deceiver, and he can drive us to act irrationally against others, all while diverting our focus from the real source of the problem, which is the spiritual warfare at play.

The enemy's primary tactic is to incite offense. This is why we must renew our minds with God's Word daily, not just on Sunday mornings but every day. The issue is personal, and we must take responsibility for our own flawed thinking patterns.

It starts with us, not by pointing fingers at others. We are all engaged in a spiritual battle, so let's put on our spiritual armor and wage this war accordingly. Realize that war is a reality, and to emerge victorious, we must fight it in the right way. We need to understand our adversary and the spiritual nature of the conflict. Our battle is not against flesh and blood.

Do we have faith in God's Word? Rather than confronting the spirit of darkness, people are engaging in conflict with each other. It's essential to stress: *stop fighting with one another!* Fighting does not lead to solutions and only adds to our collective suffering. Shooting one another, fighting, taking legal action, or incarcerating each other will not bring about real change.

While God's people are entangled in an internal struggle with their own flesh, they often fail to see that the adversary is busy scheming against them.

Why engage in battles when Jesus has already fought and emerged victorious for the entire world? The enemy can only harm us if we allow it. We may sing songs like "I'm on the battlefield for my Lord," but in reality, we find ourselves battling for our own interests in the flesh. However, the true battle is spiritual, not physical.

The adversary delights in this confusion! It's not about us personally; it's about what dwells within us. We each have a purpose, and the Holy Spirit resides within us. That's what the adversary is after— your purpose, not your skin color. The obsession with skin color is a smokescreen, diverting attention from the fact that he's undermining us in the spiritual realm while we engage in conflicts based on external appearances.

The enemy seizes his opportunity while you're focused on outward factors or the color of someone else's skin. That's why when you finally take a moment to reflect, you may find your family facing turmoil, your relationships strained, your spiritual life neglected, and your love and prayers diminished. I'm not trying to be pessimistic, but I'm merely highlighting the cunning tactics of the adversary, who uses diversions to weaken us. It's crucial to maintain our focus; the battle is perpetual in the spiritual realm, and to emerge victorious, we must understand who and what we're up against.

Consider the spirit of Jezebel! Within the Body of Christ, this spirit seeks to disrupt connections, manipulate leaders and members, and undermine God's people. It's essential to exercise discernment. How can Jesus be racist when His essence is love? It's impossible!

So, how can we exhibit racism if we are God's children? The answer lies in the condition of our hearts. The human heart is inherently flawed and can produce ungodly attitudes. Thus, we must continually guard our hearts.

 Above all else, guard your heart, for everything you do flows from it.

PROVERBS 4:23 NIV

Is it acceptable for me to be open and vulnerable right now? Did any of us choose to be who we are? Did we have any say in selecting our parents, our hair color, our eye color, or the shade of our skin? The answer to all these questions is a resounding *no*.

I can confidently answer for you, just as I can answer for myself. You see, my Father, Jesus Christ, created me and placed me in my mother's womb without soliciting my input. God doesn't require or seek our opinions in these matters.

Let that parallel sink in, for it is strikingly accurate. None of us had the power to preordain our destiny, our life, our purpose, our calling, our physical appearance, our ethnicity, or anything else for that matter. It was all bestowed upon us by God, and unfortunately, some of us have twisted this divine gift by harboring disdain for what God has created in others.

According to the Bible, everything that God created was not just good but very good. Therefore, disliking someone because of their skin color is akin to telling God that His creation is somehow inadequate. Racism is, at its core, a manifestation of hatred in its purest form.

Imagine how dull our world would be if everyone looked the same. When I visit a car dealership and see a row of identical cars, I leave, for there's little diversity. The same principle applies to people. We need a spectrum of skin tones, body shapes, sizes, hair and eye colors, heights, ages, and degrees of beauty in the world. Otherwise, life would be incredibly monotonous.

The devil's mission is to kill, steal, and destroy. Don't let him rob you of your mental peace, your time, or your God-given destiny and purpose by wasting your time on hating those who are different from you. Who said you can't have it all and be extraordinary at the same time? Society may have taught us that an attractive woman must be tall, extremely thin, and blonde, but that's entirely incorrect.

Part of the problem in our culture is that beauty comes in diverse shapes, sizes, and colors. What truly matters is a person's character and inner qualities. As Believers, our character should always reflect the heart of Jesus Christ.

 Therefore, if any man is in Christ, he is a new creature: old things are passed away, behold, all things become new.

2 CORINTHIANS 5:17 KJV

As we invite Jesus into our hearts and yield to the Holy Spirit, we become a new creation. The old self fades away, and we are reborn.

MOMENT OF REFLECTION

Psalm 51:10–11 says, "Create in me a clean heart, O God: and renew a right spirit within me. Cast me not away from thy presence: and take

not thy holy spirit from me." Meditate on this truth and journal what
God reveals to you.

_____

_____

_____

_____

_____

_____

_____

_____

_____

_____

_____

_____

_____

_____

_____

_____

_____

_____

_____

_____

_____

_____

_____

_____

_____

_____

_____

_____

_____

_____

_____

_____

_____

_____

promote harmony in the body of christ

The Lord does not see male or female. So, why would the Lord consider the color of one's skin when determining blessings or status as His child when He doesn't regard gender?

Color is only skin-deep. It is merely a superficial trait. After all, God is our Creator, so why would He ever condemn us based on something as arbitrary as skin color? Believing in one's superiority over another due to skin tone is not only absurd, but also heinous. It's crucial to realize that this notion is not from the Holy Spirit but rather from the enemy.

Jesus doesn't see the world as we do. His focus lies squarely on the heart, where true intentions reside. He looks within, while humanity tends to emphasize external appearances. This is a significant factor contributing to the current state of affairs. Unfortunately, some misguided leaders have made remarks concerning my skin tone, insinuating that my experiences as a Caucasian somehow lack depth. It's truly astonishing.

It would be irrational to think that the adversary is preoccupied with the color of our skin. He is, undeniably, a spiritual entity. My friend, the enemy couldn't care less about the shade of your skin; his sole focus is on gaining control of your soul. It's essential to recognize that this is the case. Moreover, certain leaders have assumed that I do not receive messages from God. I implore you to exercise great caution.

In His Word, God has explicitly stated, "Do not touch my anointed ones, and do my prophets no harm" (Psalm 105:15). My response to these individuals is one of prayer, for it appears they may not fully comprehend the gravity of their actions.

It's impossible for us to discern the full extent of someone's life experiences based solely on the color of their skin or their physical appearance. What some may overlook is that we all carry spiritual conflicts, scars, and wounds that are invisible to human eyes, as they exist in the realm of the spirit. The adversary engages us in spiritual battles, and there are times when we endure seasons of profound torment in the spiritual realm.

The core issue often lies in the inability of some individuals to hear from God. If both parties maintain an intimate relationship with God, have direct communion with Him through the Holy Spirit, and share a common faith in Christ, the question arises: Why is there a struggle to perceive one another in the spiritual realm? Why the difficulty in recognizing each other's identity in Christ?

It's crucial to understand that the Holy Spirit is far from foolish. He will never guide you to treat others unkindly or to single them out based on their outward differences. Absolutely not! Therefore, it's essential to exercise caution when allowing personal judgments to override the leading of the Holy Spirit within you. When someone speaks into your life, their words should align with what the Lord is conveying, rather than reflecting their own opinions or biases at the time.

I take a firm stand against every curse, negative word, slanderous utterance, deceitful expression, and demonic proclamation that may have been spoken over your life. In the mighty Name of Jesus, I declare them obliterated. In the powerful Name of Jesus, I replace these harmful words with the peace of God, His boundless love, the wisdom and knowledge that flow from Him, and the unwavering promises of our Heavenly Father.

We all have much to discover, and if we don't promptly get out of our own way, time may slip away. Some challenges simply cannot be overcome without the aid of prayer and fasting. As God's children, it's imperative that we not only recognize but fully comprehend the nature of the battles we are engaged in.

We often find ourselves pointing fingers at each other when it's the adversary's schemes and the crafty concealment of his actions. But you know what? That's precisely what he wants us to do— blame one another. When we engage in blame, we become fixated on the offense, which in turn allows the adversary to wreak havoc by diverting our focus. We end up acting in the flesh rather than the spirit. When our gaze shifts away from Jesus, we open the door to wrath, discord, resentment, and hatred, gradually hardening our hearts.

As we attend church, the Word may fall upon hearts hardened like stone. And as a result, the adversary snatches the Word away. As the cycle persists, it leaves us wondering where it got us. The adversary excels at deceiving and leading us astray, which is precisely why we need the Holy Spirit to serve as our guide and sound the alarm when the enemy plots. The adversary seeks to trap us in a never-ending cycle— attend church and leave unchanged.

When will we take the initiative to seek God's presence for ourselves? The problem lies in placing the sole responsibility of hearing from and praying to God on our leaders! No! That mindset has to stop. Regardless of whether it's your leader or not, you have no assurance they are praying for you. Because this is a deeply personal matter, each of us must cultivate our individual prayer life and foster our relationship with our Heavenly Father.

The Holy Spirit yearns for a close, intimate relationship with each of His children. Just because my three adult children are now grown doesn't mean I no longer desire to have a close connection with them. It's actually quite the opposite! I remain deeply interested in their lives, progress, dreams, and aspirations. I'm committed to doing everything in my power to support, encourage, and propel them toward their destinies. The same holds true for our Heavenly Father! Since the Holy Spirit resides within us, we can reach out to Him whenever we desire! He truly cares for us and wants to have a relationship with us.

MOMENT OF REFLECTION

Psalm 27:8 says, "My heart says of you, 'Seek his face!' Your face, Lord, I will seek." Meditate on this truth and journal what God reveals to you.

_____

_____

_____

_____

_____

_____

_____

_____

_____

_____

_____

_____

_____

_____

_____

_____

_____

_____

_____

_____

embrace the holy spirit

Fight in the spirit, and you will conquer! When you contend with mere flesh and blood, defeat is certain. The adversary preys on your reluctance to engage in the spiritual fight! Our words hold immense influence. God spoke, and there was light. The tongue's power dictates life and death.

 Whatever a man saith so is he, for as he thinks in his heart, so is he: Eat and drink, saith he to thee: but his heart is not with thee. Life and death are in the power of the tongue.

PROVERBS 23:7 KJV

The words you speak have the power to shape your reality! It's a guaranteed investment! Every time you speak, you're making deposits into your account, influencing your environment, your present, and your future. It will inevitably manifest. Some of us don't need to wait for the devil to hatch schemes against us; we inadvertently do it to ourselves with our own words!

When we encounter words spoken over us that we discern are not aligned with God's truth, it's our duty to nullify those words and declare what God affirms about us. Allowing others to dictate our narrative grants them undue sway over our lives, and this isn't in accordance with God's divine plan. God knows what's best for each of us, and His voice should be our guiding light.

The adversary, at times, masquerades as the Holy Spirit, mimicking His voice. This is why the Bible encourages us to discern the spirits by testing them. We occasionally give the devil more credit than he deserves. You can give yourself a pat on the back, for it's our own words that sometimes work against us when we should be proclaiming God's Word and breathing life into situations instead of speaking death. The enemy can't accomplish anything unless permitted.

Upon evaluating your life, you'll come to recognize the stories you've been narrating to yourself. You also have the capacity to influence the narratives that others bring into their lives. It's not uncommon for certain parents to make declarations such as "My son is troublesome," "My children are unruly," or "My daughter is troublesome." But here's the catch: if you persistently utter these negative affirmations, you'll inadvertently shape your children into being just that – disobedient and challenging. As parents, you are intended to serve as their guiding lights, their protectors. Thus, it's imperative to speak life into their existence, imparting blessings for their futures.

Speak forth what you aspire to witness! Regardless of how circumstances may appear, refrain from echoing negativity. Instead, speak life, prosperity, blessings, and God's favor over your life and the lives of your family.

Don't glance at the issue and immediately begin stating what you observe! As God's children, our journey is not governed by what we see, but rather by our unwavering faith. Faith is the manifestation of things hoped for, the proof of things unseen! It's faith that we should uphold.

Where has your trust gone? Some of us are completely blinded by what we see! Take note of this fact! When adversity assails my life, I abstain from speaking about it; instead, I plead the Blood of Jesus!

 Now we have received not the spirit of the world, but the Spirit which is of God, so that we might know the things that are freely given to us by God.

1 CORINTHIANS 2:12 KJV

When we speak the incorrect thing over our lives, we give the devil a bat to smash us over the head with. We're essentially handing him ammunition to use against us. It's crucial not to share all our dreams and visions with just anyone because, believe it or not, there are times when they might actually pray against us. When you vocalize your aspirations to someone who isn't in your corner, the adversary takes note and begins scheming to thwart your vision and hinder your goals. Why? Because he's well aware that your success would make you an unstoppable force, a living testament to the reality and trustworthiness of God!

Our love for Him should be born out of gratitude for His boundless kindness and grace. It truly troubles me when some churches host events and invite others to join, yet when the tables turn, they hesitate to provide support. That is discrimination! That is not love; that is selfishness! I'm just going to tell it how it is!

You see, I've been anointed with a gift of correction, and it allows me to perceive things differently. I grasp the spirit and motivation behind these actions. Unfortunately, many churches today are in disarray, with some being even worse than the world at large. Some churchgoers look down on people living on the streets as if they're superior, forgetting that we all have a past.

We can't pretend we've always been saved. The church, as a whole, seems to have lost its way. It's become more of a corporation or organization when it should be a living, breathing organism. Jesus won't return for a church service or a building; He's coming back for a church without blemish. We've seen pastors and leaders committing reprehensible acts within the church, and it's a tragedy.

How can we draw the world if we still enjoy it? We need to seek deliverance from these destructive influences and strive to walk upright before God. When the leadership is tainted, the entire body suffers. We need Jesus!

Programs wouldn't be necessary if we all faithfully tithed and gave offerings. I'm not here to condemn churches, just to speak what I believe is the truth. Our light can't shine if we're living in sin. Unfortunately, racism and other issues persist even within the Body of Christ.

The Body of Christ appears sluggish, often seeing but not truly comprehending. Your response to a crisis says a lot about your faith. Most of us aren't truly led by the Holy Spirit; instead, we walk around carrying offenses, ready to gossip at the slightest provocation. This is the behavior that must stop.

MOMENT OF REFLECTION

Ephesians 4:29 says, "Do not let any unwholesome talk come out of your mouths, but only what is helpful for building others up according to their needs, that it may benefit those who listen." Meditate on this truth and journal what God reveals to you.

_____

_____

_____

_____

_____

_____

_____

_____

_____

discard labels

People in this world just love to put labels on things. Even in the Body of Christ, we're no exception. These labels make people feel like they've got some kind of power, as if they're better than the person standing right next to them. You've heard them all – white supremacy, black supremacy, black love, black power, white power. But let me tell you, these labels don't give you any real power; they're just a different kind of trap. They do nothing but divide us, and that's exactly what the enemy wants. These labels hint at something deeper, something that's all about focusing on ourselves. However, that's not what God is all about!

You see, the real power, the one that can truly save you and transform your life, comes from one source only – the power of the Holy Spirit. All these other labels are just human-made categories and groups. God has nothing to do with them. But when you come to Christ, your label gets a major upgrade! You're not just labeled as anything else; you're labeled as a child of God!

You've been branded by Jesus' Blood! You're labeled with favor and grace. You're marked as cherished, beloved, and precious in His sight. You're labeled as royalty, anointed, gifted, talented, a disciple, a prophet, a minister, an intercessor, blessed, and highly favored – praise God for that!

So when that enemy looks at you, he doesn't see just you; he sees Jesus' Blood all over you – he sees *red!* I'd rather the devil see Jesus' Blood all over me than me. That's how he knows you've been marked.

What about all those other labels the world wants to place on you? They're fake, and even the ones you put on yourself – they're just as fake! You're more than just 'black love' or 'white power.' To act right, we've got to get real about who we are. This world isn't our permanent home; we're just passing through, so why get all worked up about someone else's skin color when they're leaving this world just like you are?

We're getting new bodies someday, and who knows what color they'll be? Does it even matter? Nope! My mission is to bring glory to my Father and help establish His Kingdom. So we've got to humble ourselves before God and turn away from our own evil ways.

Instead of constantly asking God for stuff – houses, cars, better jobs, husbands, wives, etc. – we should be asking for deliverance. Most people are begging for things that'll eventually fade away and won't mean a thing when Jesus returns. Even if you've got the Holy Spirit, you'll still need deliverance.

What we should be wishing for is eternity with Jesus in Heaven. Lots of God's children live defeated lives because they've never really basked in His presence. We need that close relationship with our Heavenly Father, and with the Holy Spirit— it's totally possible! We need to take the time to get to know Him, to repent, and to learn from Him. When we do, we'll start to take on the mind, heart, and love of Christ. That's what it's all about.

~

MOMENT OF REFLECTION

1 Samuel 16:7 says, "But the Lord said to Samuel, 'Do not consider his appearance or his height, for I have rejected him. The Lord does not

look at the things people look at. People look at the outward appearance, but the Lord looks at the heart." Meditate on this truth and journal what God reveals to you.

_____

_____

_____

_____

_____

_____

_____

_____

_____

_____

_____

_____

_____

_____

_____

_____

_____

_____

_____

_____

_____

_____

_____

_____

_____

_____

_____

_____

_____

_____

_____

_____

develop your relationship with the holy spirit

To stay ahead of the adversary, it's essential to maintain a consistent prayer life and establish a close connection with the Holy Spirit. Our relationship with the Holy Spirit should be so intimate that we can recognize the adversary's presence before he strikes!

Now, you might be wondering what this means. It means that the Holy Spirit will reveal to you or inform you about the adversary's schemes in advance, enabling you to intercede and pray against them in Jesus' Name! This is what I mean by detecting the adversary before his arrival! This is what we call spiritual warfare! We can use the Seed to wage war against the enemy.

The Seed signifies the Gospel of God's Kingdom. A seed can be planted on one of four types of ground:

1. The first seed sowed fell on (hardened) soil and had no fruit.
2. The second seed was planted in (rocky) soil and yielded fruit for a brief period.
3. The third seed was planted in (thorny) soil and produced fruit for a brief period.

4. The fourth seed was planted in (excellent) soil and yielded three different amounts of fruit: thirty, sixty, and a hundredfold.

There is only one seed and four soils: "The Story of the Sewer." In this story, the soil is referred to as the heart. What is the state of our hearts?

> When anyone hears the message (word) about the kingdom and does not understand it, the evil one comes and snatches away what was sown in his heart. This is the seed sown along the path.

MATTHEW 13:19 KJV

When will we wake up and acknowledge that we are currently engaged in a spiritual battle, one that requires spiritual insight and discernment to emerge victorious? Instead of battling our real adversary, we often find ourselves fighting amongst ourselves, getting sidetracked in the process. It's crucial to resist these distractions!

The adversary frequently sends individuals into our lives to divert our attention away from the Holy Spirit. Conversely, when God intends to bless us, He brings people into our lives for that very purpose. We need to be vigilant, prayerful, and attuned to God's Kingdom and His holiness. This will enable us to discern the origin and purpose of those who enter our lives and guide our responses accordingly.

I feel great frustration when I witness a child of God engaging in battles with mere human beings. This is not the conflict we should be involved in! Such conflicts are like futile attempts to move forward when our wheels are stuck in the mud.

We must remember that God is the creator of everything and everyone. According to the Bible, He formed us and placed us in our mother's womb with meticulous care, shaping us according to His divine plan. He endowed us with unique abilities, talents, and personalities, all carefully crafted by His loving hands. It's truly remarkable!

> For you formed my inward part: you knitted me together in my mother's womb. I praise you, for I am fearfully and wonderfully made. Wonderful are your works: my soul knows it very well. My frame was not hidden from you, when I was being made in secret, intricately woven in the depth of the earth. Your eyes saw my unformed substance: in your book were written, every one of them, the days that were formed for me, when as yet there was none of them.
>
> JOB 3:13–16 KJV

Isn't it remarkable that he took the time to offer us these things to help us become the people we are today? He made you and me, so when we hate one other, we essentially hate what He created.

> Thus says the Lord, your Redeemer, who formed you from the womb: I am the Lord, who made all things, who above stretched out the heavens, who spread out the earth by myself.
>
> JOB 3:24 KJV

Some of us behave and interact with others as if we are the architects of our own existence, but this couldn't be further from the truth. We didn't create ourselves; it was God who brought everything into being!

Let's raise our voices in praise and gratitude to His holy name! To truly understand Him and fulfill His divine purpose for our lives, we need to shift our focus away from self-centeredness. Some of us waste our precious time on frivolous pursuits.

I want to assure you that when Jesus returns, the color of some-one's skin or any other such distinctions will not be a concern. He has made it clear in His word that His return will be sudden, like a thief in the night. His message also emphasizes that when He does return, we should continue in our righteous endeavors because it will be too late to make amends.

In essence, He is returning for His church, which is us. Are you prepared? Can you confidently say you'd go with Jesus if He returned today? He promised in His word that He has prepared a place for us, and in His Father's house, there are many mansions awaiting us. I'm eagerly anticipating my mansion and my crown! Hallelujah!

The Church has a significant role to play in advancing the King-dom, yet many are not actively engaged. While some focus on events and fundraisers, there's a pressing need for ministry. What about the homeless, the residents of care facilities, the youth, and the broken marriages? What about the responsibility to educate and counsel God's children?

Sometimes, leaders can't offer guidance because they too are grap-pling with personal challenges and lack the authority to effect change. We're all human, but if we aspire to serve in ministry, we must first heal ourselves so that we can minister effectively without causing harm.

Churches may be bustling with programs and performances, but what about the salvation of souls? There's a disturbing trend of churches hosting impromptu events to overshadow other planned programs, solely to prevent their congregation from attending else-where. This divisive behavior is far from God's desire!

We must remember that we share one faith and one body, and our worship should unite us rather than divide us. Ministry transcends pulpit preaching; it involves being the hands and feet of Christ, sharing His love and compassion with those in need, and introducing Jesus to those who have yet to know Him. To truly demonstrate love, we need Jesus in our hearts!

MOMENT OF REFLECTION

1 John 4:11 says, "Dear friends, since God so loved us, we also ought to love one another." Meditate on this truth and journal what God reveals to you.

_____

_____

_____

_____

_____

_____

_____

_____

_____

_____

_____

_____

_____

_____

_____

_____

_____

_____

_____

_____

_____

_____

_____

_____

_____

_____

_____

_____

_____

_____

reject the spirit of division

Allowing ourselves to take offense can hinder our effectiveness; offense can kill your fruit. To be clear, many ministries are doing incredible work for Jesus. However, just like any other human institution, the body of Christ is not without its imperfections. It is essential to cultivate virtues such as patience, self-control, and a slow-to-anger attitude. Both are listed as part of the fruit of the Spirit.

 But the fruit of the Spirit is love, joy, peace, patience, kindness, goodness, faithfulness, gentleness, and self-control.

GALATIANS 5:22–23 NIV

The Body of Christ has experienced division. If we desire to make a positive impact on the world, we must first work on self-improvement. Our strength is magnified when we collaborate.

As God's children and leaders, it is essential that we awaken and cultivate spiritual discernment. This will enable us to pray, fast, and intercede for a world in crisis.

Leaders cannot entirely escape the influence of their environment. Every day, the world becomes increasingly challenging. It's time to reconcile with God and immerse ourselves in Jesus.

Attending church services should not merely be for our amusement. Regrettably, in many instances, we experience neglect and mistreatment within the church. Our purpose in attending should be to seek, praise, and adore God for who He is rather than seeking only what He can do for us.

The role of the shepherd is to feed the sheep, and the sheep should diligently receive God's message, allowing it to penetrate their souls and equip them to minister to a suffering world.

However, this is often not the case. We may attend church to experience emotional highs, briefly forget our problems, shed tears, and then return to the same challenges we face in our daily lives. This is akin to using the Holy Spirit for a temporary emotional escape. We should seek genuine deliverance, not just the sensation of it. It is unreasonable to expect the pastor to take on the entire burden.

We are God's army, being trained for ministry, not for a worldly life with worldly thinking. While we may attend church to sing praises to the Lord, our focus should be on living and walking in the Spirit.

What exactly does this mean? We should cultivate a deep relationship with the Holy Spirit, immerse ourselves in His Word, pray, and meditate on it. This process allows the Word to soften our hardened hearts and transform us into fertile ground. It prevents the adversary from snatching the Word away as soon as it is sown. We should let the Word be written on our hearts, making it readily available when needed.

How does one draw fresh water from a dry well? Our inner rivers of living water should flow like a continuous stream! Some individuals attend church simply because it seems like the right thing to do. However, living for Jesus encompasses much more!

The church holds a communal responsibility. The church should be a model for its community. This includes addressing issues like racism. Remember, you are the church!

Our entire lives should be dedicated to worshipping the Lord.

When we prioritize seeking His Kingdom and His righteousness, everything else will fall into place.

We are not meant to compare ourselves to one another, as the Bible advises against it. We are distinct!

 Don't compare yourself with others. Just look at your work to see if you have done anything to be proud of. You must each accept the responsibilities that are yours. Whoever is being taught god's word should share the good things they have with the one who is teaching them.

GALATIANS 6:4–6 ERV

We are His cherished ones! In His eyes, we are priceless! For us, He paid the ultimate price! It's simple when you think about it. God made us for a specific reason. He is greater than the world's occupants.

 Whenever the living creatures give glory, honor, and thanks to him who sits on the throne and who lives forever and ever. The twenty-four elders fall before him who sits on the throne and worship him who lives forever and ever. They lay their crowns before the throne and say. 'You are worthy, our Lord and God, to receive glory and honor and power, for you created all things, and by your will, they were created and have their being.'

REVELATION 4:9–11 NIV

We've been created for a divine reason. Inside of every one of us is a sense of purpose. We have responsibilities that we must fulfill. We are a unique people, a royal priesthood, and a generation that has been selected.

 But you are a chosen people, a royal priesthood, a holy nation, God's special possession, that you may declare the praises of him who called you out of darkness into his wonderful light.

1 PETER 2:9 NIV

How can we manifest God's purpose within us if we are not filled with the Holy Spirit? The Holy Spirit is undeniably real, and we require His guidance in every facet of our lives! Hallelujah!

As a society, we have become so self-absorbed that we often struggle to see beyond our own interests. When we are constantly distracted, it becomes challenging to recognize if the adversary is launching an attack on us. The enemy will employ every tactic at his disposal to divert our attention from our divine calling.

Our primary purpose is to worship God. How can we fulfill this mission if we harbor resentment toward others due to differences in skin color? I cannot stress enough the importance of understanding that our battle is against spiritual principalities in dark places, not against fellow human beings.

We are engaged in a spiritual warfare, not a physical one. Our true adversary is the devil, not one another. This understanding is essential for us to engage in effective and victorious spiritual warfare.

Over two thousand years ago, Jesus triumphed over the devil on the cross. So why do we persist in living defeated lives when He already conquered everything, including racism, on the cross? The answer lies in our failure to grasp who we are and to whom we belong.

When we accept Jesus as our Lord and Savior, we become His children. In fact, we are already His beloved children before accepting Him, as He has already accepted us. All we need to do is reciprocate that acceptance.

Jesus came to save a world in peril, including sinners like you and me. He came to grant us abundant life. Yet when we allow the enemy to infiltrate our lives and introduce other spirits, we live in defeat rather than victory.

The devil is a cunning deceiver who can lead us to believe we are right when, in fact, we are falling into his snares. He engages us in mental games, ultimately benefiting himself.

The devil may entice us onto a precarious limb and then abandon us, leaving us stranded when the limb breaks. His goal is to keep us from occupying our rightful place. In truth, we have a heavenly seat with Christ Jesus!

MOMENT OF REFLECTION

1 Corinthians 1:10 says, "I appeal to you, brothers and sisters, in the name of our Lord Jesus Christ, that all of you agree with one another in what you say and that there be no divisions among you, but that you be perfectly united in mind and thought." Meditate on this truth and journal what God reveals to you.

_____

_____

_____

_____

_____

_____

_____

_____

_____

_____

_____

_____

_____

speak the word over yourself

Make it a steadfast practice to pray Psalm 91 over yourself and your loved ones each day, for it serves as a divine canopy of protection. This powerful psalm offers a profound sense of security and assurance, reminding us of God's unwavering presence and watchful care.

As you engage in this daily prayer, immerse yourself in the words of Psalm 91, allowing its promises to envelop your spirit. Begin by acknowledging God as your refuge and fortress, the One in whom you trust without reservation. Declare His role as your shelter, your safe haven from life's storms.

Visualize the protective wings of the Almighty, under which you and your family find refuge. As you recite the psalm, believe in the faithfulness of God's promises, that He will deliver you from perilous situations, shield you from harm, and send His angels to guard your path.

Embrace the idea that no fear should grip your heart, for the Lord is your stronghold. Through this daily practice, cultivate a deep sense of intimacy with God, knowing that His presence is a shield of defense around you.

Praying Psalm 91 is not merely a ritual but an act of unwavering faith. It is a declaration of trust in the God who watches over His children, keeping them safe from harm's way. As you speak these words, envision yourself and your family dwelling securely under the divine canopy of protection that Psalm 91 provides, and rest in the assurance that God is your refuge and fortress, now and forever.

> He who dwells in the shelter of the Most High will rest in the shadow of the Almighty. I will say of the LORD, 'He is my refuge and my fortress, my God, in whom I trust.' Surely he will save you from the fowler's snare and from the deadly pestilence. He will cover you with his feathers, and under his wings you will find refuge; his faithfulness will be your shield and rampart. You will not fear the terror of night, nor the arrow that flies by day, nor the pestilence that stalks in the darkness, nor the plague that destroys at midday. A thousand may fall at your side, ten thousand at your right hand, but it will not come near you. You will only observe with your eyes and see the punishment of the wicked. If you make the Most High your dwelling— even the LORD, who is my refuge— then no harm will befall you, no disaster will come near your tent. For he will command his angels concerning you to guard you in all your ways; they will lift you up in their hands, so that you will not strike your foot against a stone. You will tread upon the lion and the cobra; you will trample the great lion and the serpent. 'Because he loves me,' says the LORD, "I will rescue him; I will protect him, for he acknowledges my name. He will call upon me, and I will answer him; I will be with him in trouble, I will deliver him and honor him. With long life will I satisfy him and show him my salvation.

PSALM 91:1-16 NIV

MOMENT OF REFLECTION

2 Corinthians 4:13 says, "It is written: 'I believed; therefore, I have spoken.'" Since we have that same spirit of faith, we also believe and therefore speak." Meditate on this truth and journal what God reveals to you.

_____

_____

_____

_____

_____

_____

_____

_____

_____

_____

_____

_____

_____

_____

_____

_____

_____

_____

_____

_____

_____

_____

_____

receive grace

We are engaged in a spiritual battle against forces in high places, darkness, wickedness, and the devil himself—not against each other. Only when we recognize this truth can we fully understand our adversary and engage in the right fight!

I pray, in the Name of Jesus, for unity within the Body of Christ to put an end to racism. Our strength lies in our unity, not in division. Together, we are strong, but apart, we are weak. We must come together, for Jesus has already paid the price and publicly defeated the devil.

We are conquerors in multiple ways, but when will we truly believe it? When will we accept God's word and have faith in what He says? It's time for us to celebrate our victories!

We have already triumphed because Jesus triumphed on the cross! When the devil thought he was defeating Jesus, he was, in fact, defeated himself.

This realization may become clearer to some of you later: everything was nailed to the Cross, and Jesus conquered it there. Some of you may not realize that you're fighting a battle that's already been won!

The enemy wants you to believe that you must achieve certain things to win, but it's already done. On the Cross, Jesus paid the penalty for every sin in full, enabling us to live a victorious, sin-free life!

Jesus willingly gave His life because He cares deeply for us. No one forcibly took His life; He laid it down willingly. No one can take Jesus Christ's life; He had to offer it willingly.

I pray that this revelation transforms your life. Jesus is grace personified. To receive and apply grace, we must live by it and extend it to others, even when they hurt us.

I once asked God for a deeper understanding of grace so that I could fully apply it in my life and toward others. One day, when someone questioned my past, I responded calmly, untroubled by their accusations. I couldn't understand why I wasn't angry with them, and God revealed that I was forgiven for all my sins and living in His grace. The Holy Spirit reassured me that the past they were trying to condemn me for no longer belonged to me; it was covered by grace!

Our sins are wiped away when we invite Jesus into our hearts and repent. They no longer define us; instead, they belong to Jesus. He takes our sin and exchanges it for His grace. Those sins are no longer associated with us! Thank you, Jesus!

MOMENT OF REFLECTION

Colossians 3:13 says, "Bear with each other and forgive one another if any of you has a grievance against someone. Forgive as the Lord forgave you." Meditate on this truth and journal what God reveals to you.

_____

_____

_____

_____

_____

accept diversity

It's not just about African Americans. God's children are all royalty, regardless of their ethnicity. In Christ Jesus, there is no division! Jesus loves us all equally, and we should reciprocate that love by treating each other equally.

The choice is simple: are you on the side of the devil or on God's side? I firmly believe that God chose me to write this book because of my purpose in Him. At times, I may come across as direct and even harsh, but there are certain truths that need to be spoken and brought to light. These truths reveal the spiritual aspects of our lives and remind us that we're all in this battle together.

As the Bible says, 'I have lured many with love.' But how can the body of Christ attract people if we are divided, segregated, and at odds with one another? Baptists don't want to worship with Methodists, and Methodists don't want to worship with Pentecostals. Is this really the unity Jesus intended for His followers?

Who are we to assume that we are superior to others or that we have all the answers? Who are we to pass judgment on anyone? The truth is, we've all sinned and fallen short of God's glory.

To grow and mature spiritually, we need deliverance. We need deliverance to walk in His will and His ways, and we need it to guide others toward deliverance. Deliverance involves spiritual warfare, and we must actively pursue it.

If you operate in a spirit and allow it to persist in your life, you can expect the adversary to wreak havoc. However, we should never willingly give the adversary authority over our lives when we have the power of our Heavenly Father through Jesus Christ, who died on the cross over two thousand years ago to give us life more abundantly.

We should not let racism or any form of hatred persist in our lives. We need to take a good look in the mirror and examine the fruit we bear. Ask yourself if you are genuinely content with who you are, how you treat people, and how you interact with those who are different from you.

This is a personal journey. When we pass away, we will meet our Creator alone. At that moment, the color of someone's skin won't matter. Let's pause and reflect on racism. Why are we afraid of someone simply because of their skin color?

Fear drives us to commit terrible acts, while faith is its antithesis. Fear destroys faith, but faith cancels out fear. Our nation is currently plagued by an atmosphere of offense.

Jesus warned us about offense when it comes to the adversary. We must not allow ourselves to be offended. Offense is a deception used by the adversary to hinder our spiritual fruit. So, pray that you remain unoffended, as offense suffocates the fruit.

 Good sense makes one slow to anger, and it is his glory to overlook an offense.

PROVERBS 19:11 ESV

 And blessed is the one who is not offended by me.

LUKE 7:23 ESV

Wake up and know who and what we are truly fighting! If we are all God's children, why can't we come together in worship? It's time we get ourselves in order!

MOMENT OF REFLECTION

John 16:33 says, "I have said these things to you, that in me you may have peace. In the world, you will have tribulation. But take heart: I have overcome the world." Meditate on this truth and journal what God reveals to you.

_____

_____

_____

_____

_____

_____

_____

_____

_____

_____

_____

_____

_____

_____

_____

_____

_____

_____

_____

_____

_____

_____

renew your mind

T his book is covered by the redeeming blood of Jesus. My
prayer is that it will be a catalyst for life-changing transformation. The Holy Spirit led me to write this book, speaking
through its pages. In Jesus' Name, I urge you to pay close attention to
every word, as I believe it will greatly benefit your life.

I have an immense love for both Jesus and humanity. Let's come
together and make a positive impact on the world. This mission was
imparted to me by the Holy Spirit, and it's only the beginning.

The purpose of this book isn't to generate profits. Its mission is to
open your eyes, examine your heart, and awaken you from spiritual
slumber. It's time to realize that everything God created, including
each of us, is excellent and very good.

Let us not disapprove of God's creation. My prayer is that all who
read this book will grasp the profound messages conveyed by the Holy
Spirit.

I didn't come here to make friends or tell you what you want to
hear. I'm here to fulfill the Lord's work and dismantle the devil's
strongholds. My purpose is to empower, educate, and awaken you.

I pray that everyone turns away from their sinful ways and begins to love others more profoundly. Let there be healing and transformation in your hearts.

In the mighty Name of Jesus, I pray that the Word of God renews your mind and brings healing. Love has the power to cover a multitude of sins, and God is love. God's love transcends human distinctions, for love has no color.

People often label themselves as significant. Let's move beyond superficial feelings that deceive us. This country needs love and unity more than ever.

Love one another as He first loved you. He loves you dearly. This is America, the Land of the Free, the Home of the Brave, and we trust in God. However, recent events have shown that we must examine our hearts. How can we degrade fellow Americans based on their differences? How can we perpetrate harm based on skin color? This is unacceptable and treacherous. We are all God's creations, uniquely formed and placed in our mother's womb by His design. Everything about us, including our skin color, is part of God's plan.

So I have to ask you a question: do you consider yourself to be above God? Racism tells God that He made a mistake when it comes to someone's skin tone.

It's astonishing how easily people let the adversary use them. Remember, we were all created by God and born into this world through women, with the same basic physiology.

Let us examine our hearts and invite the Holy Spirit to fill us with God's love. May we receive His love and allow the Holy Spirit to guide us.

With God's love, I love you! May God bless you and your family. Always remember, racism is a devilish spirit; let Jesus' Blood cleanse and protect you.

Pray for our country to unite in prayer and for our youth, as they are the future. We are the pioneers, responsible for paving the way for future generations. Break the cycle of generational curses and let the Holy Spirit heal your heart. Racism, like any other spirit, can be passed from generation to generation. Break this cycle now in Jesus' mighty Name.

Today, check your heart, ask Jesus to cleanse it, and seek His forgiveness. Request the heart of Christ to be within you, so you may be transformed. Allow the Holy Spirit to heal your heart, cast out the spirit of racism, and any seeds it may have sown. Jesus is the way, the truth, and the life. Without Him, we can do nothing.

May God bless us all!

MOMENT OF REFLECTION

Psalm 139:23-24 says, "Search me, God, and know my heart; test me and know my anxious thoughts. See if there is any offensive way in me and lead me in the way everlasting." Meditate on this truth and journal what God reveals to you.

_____

_____

_____

_____

_____

_____

_____

_____

_____

_____

_____

_____

_____

_____

_____

_____

_____

_____

final words

I choose to walk in purpose to fulfill the calling on my life! I'm immensely thankful to God for giving me a heart filled with love for others. Allowing the adversary to use you for his purposes is not a wise decision!

In the mighty Name of Jesus, I denounce, paralyze, and eradicate the spirit of racism! I will combat it with the power of the blood of Jesus and dismantle all its works! In the glorious Name of Jesus, I declare love, peace, joy, humility, kindness, meekness, compassion, mercy, and grace over this nation!

We are all God's children, meticulously crafted by His hands and placed in our mother's womb, created in His image. We had no say in our skin color, gender, nationality, shape, or anything else. His hands fashioned us exactly as He intended, and we are precious in His eyes.

We are priceless in the eyes of the one and only true and living God. This is astonishing, and I praise God for Jesus and Jesus for the Holy Spirit! All glory to His name.

God is magnificent, glorious, alive, and overflowing with love. He is the beginning, the end, and everything in between! Grace is not just a concept; it is embodied in a person, and that person is Jesus!

I pray that you gain a deep understanding of grace and how to apply it in your life and the lives of others. In Jesus' Name, I hope that every word in this book brings Him glory and honor!

I challenge you to renew your mind by immersing yourself in God's Word and allowing the Holy Spirit to minister to you. The Holy Spirit is an extraordinary teacher, comforter, helper, and guide to our souls.

I have attended the school of the Holy Spirit, and He will educate you about Himself, leading you to the truth, all in the Name of Jesus!

I pray that this book blesses you and ministers to your spirit, enabling you to see through the eyes of the Holy Spirit. We bear the responsibility to love one another, and by spreading love throughout the world, we can make our planet a better place!

May God's blessings pour upon you and your family! There is nothing that can deter me from loving you.

acknowledgments

I'd like to thank Bobby and Carolyn Greenwood, my father and mother. My parents are the reason I am here. I thank God for them.

I'd like to thank my apostle, Dr. Antonio Schroeder, for constantly pushing me and pronouncing God's promises over my life, as well as supporting me through the difficult times.

I'd also like to express my gratitude to the Holy Spirit for selecting me to write this book. I'm humbled and thrilled to be a part of this book and the changes it will bring to the world!

about the author

Kristina Carter is a native of Memphis, Tennessee, who now resides in Mississippi with her three children and seven grandchildren. She is a minister and a Prophet of God. Kristina is a visionary and extremely creative with multifaceted gifts.

Kristina is the founder of "Broken Wings Ministries," in which she helps young mothers furnish their first homes when venturing out on their own. She has several other ministries that she will give birth to this year. Her heart and divine passion are to help the homeless and end homelessness.

In her first book, "Skin Deep," a prophetic book that addresses the spirit of racism, she hopes to end racism worldwide— both locally and internationally.

She contributed to a magazine that uplifts and empowers single women. Having been married twice and soon to be single herself, she possesses a wealth of wisdom and seasoned experience, eagerly shining a light for other single women.

To get in contact with Kristina, you can reach her via email:
kristina8a8a@gmail.com